ISABEL THOMAS

Illustrated by **NIKALAS CATLOW**

SELF-DESTRUCTING SCIENCE

SPACE

COUNTDOWN TO SELF-DESTRUCTION

Ever dreamed of exploring space?
What do you think you'll need?

CHECKLIST

☒	☒	☒	☒	☑
Spacesuit	Rocket	Years of training	Planet-size brain	THIS BOOK AND A PAIR OF SCISSORS

Yup, your mission to space starts now! This book is packed with space activities that use every page in a different way.

It's not one of those zzzzzzzzz activity books that's all about sitting quietly and doodling. This book goes off with a BANG!

Get ready to tear, fold, cut, construct, and experiment . . . but be warned:

THIS BOOK WILL SELF-DESTRUCT!

BLOOMSBURY
Activity Books

HOW TO ~~USE~~ DESTROY THIS BOOK

Space is a big place to explore. Where will you start?

BUILD A ROCKET (PAGE 17)

GET READY FOR YOUR SPACEWALK (PAGE 28)

CHALLENGE A FRIEND TO A MARS ROVER RACE (PAGE 33)

START A COLONY OF ALIEN BUGS (PAGE 35)

OPEN A WORMHOLE AND LEAP RIGHT THROUGH (PAGE 51)

Let's go!

TRAINING CAMP

Cut along solid lines

- - - - - Fold along dashed lines

WARNING! THIS PAGE WILL SELF-DESTRUCT!

Look out for this icon—these pages will completely self-destruct, so make sure you read every word before getting started!

SAFETY INFORMATION FOR MISSION CONTROL

All the projects in this book have been designed to be safe for children to carry out at home, if they are comfortable using scissors. We recommend that an adult help with or supervise certain projects, including Gravity race (page 12), Pocket rocket (page 17), Don't get dazzled (page 22), and Keeping time (page 25). You should never look at the sun directly or with any type of binoculars or telescope. When launching the Pocket rocket (page 17), make sure that it is pointed away from other people.

Extra gear:

Most projects just use scissors, glue, and colored markers. These boxes tell you if you need to pack any extra gear.

WHERE AM I?

Our solar system is a collection of billions of rocks hurtling around the Sun. If you get lost, use this handy key to figure out what kind of rock you're standing on.

Just the Sun

What shape is it?

Lumpy

Ball-shaped

What is it made of?

Does a rock taste different if it falls to Earth?

Yes, it's a little meteor.

Do similar space rocks orbit at around the same distance from the Sun?

Ice and grit

No

Yes

PLANET

COMET

PLANETS

Planets orbit the Sun and have a round shape. They are massive enough to clear their orbits by pulling in any objects in their path—or bashing them out of the way.

Spotted and named: 8

Estimated number: 8

DWARF PLANETS

Like planets, dwarf planets are round and orbit the Sun. They are not massive enough to clear their paths around the Sun, so they share their orbits with similar objects. Most dwarf planets, including Pluto, are found beyond Neptune in the Kuiper Belt. They are also known as plutoids.

Spotted and named: 5

Estimated number: 100 or more

DWARF PLANET

No

PHEW!

OH! IT'S A NEAR-EARTH OBJECT!

So, you're stranded on a space rock. What does it orbit?

Another object as well as the Sun

Is it a natural object or made by humans?

Natural

Human-made

ock and metal

How big is it?

oulder-size or bigger

Less than three feet (1m) in diameter

How many are there just like it?

One of a kind

More than I can count

ARTIFICIAL SATELLITE

ASTEROID

Where is it?

Whizzing through space

Yikes! It crash-landed on Earth!

RING PARTICLES

METEOROID

METEORITE

MOON

MOONS

Moons may be planet-size or asteroid-size, round or lumpy, but they all orbit an object other than the Sun.

Spotted and named: 182

Estimated number: Several hundred

Does its path around the Sun cross Earth's?

ASTEROIDS

Asteroids are tiny lumps of space rubble left over from when the solar system was forming. Most orbit the Sun in a region called the asteroid belt. Although they are closer together than the planets, the average distance between asteroids is more than 600,000 miles—so flying through an asteroid field would actually be quite safe!

Spotted and named: More than 680,000

Estimated number: More than 750,000 larger than three-fifths of a mile (1 km), and millions of smaller ones

es

MAKE YOUR OWN BIG BANG(ER)

The universe is EVERYTHING there is—from giant galaxies to minuscule mites. Scientists have figured out that it all started with a huge explosion known as the Big Bang. Can you make a big bang of your own, using only this page?

Fold this page to make a paper "banger." The biggest banger ever folded like this was almost nine feet tall.

Extra gear:
· Scissors

What to do:

1. Take this page out of the book. Crease all the white dotted lines firmly and unfold.
2. Fold the four corners in to the matching symbols.
3. Fold the paper in half, so the long sides meet.
4. Bring the top points down so the folded edges meet along the blue line.
5. Turn the paper over and fold in half so the white dots meet.
6. Hold the bottom point between your thumb and forefinger. Raise your arm and move it down as quickly as possible. Listen for a big bang, and watch stars and galaxies explode from the center.

The bigger the banger, the bigger the bang!

Your banger won't work in space. Sound needs something to travel through, but space is completely empty.

WHAT WAS THE BIG BANG?

Almost 14 billion years ago, everything in the universe was squashed together into a bubble too tiny to see, and trillions of times hotter than the Sun. When the Big Bang happened, the universe began to expand and cool down very quickly. As this happened, space matter began to form, and eventually, after about 200 million years, this made the first stars. These huge nuclear reactors created the materials that make up everything else, from planets and moons to living plants and creatures.

Try making bangers out of different types of paper to find out which makes the loudest bang. Newspaper and brown packing paper give great results!

FOLD

FOLD

FOLD

FOLD

Step 6

8

NOT-SO-NEAR NEIGHBORS

They call it "space" for a reason . . . the distances between planets are huge. This page turns into a handy scale map of the solar system, to help you work out how many sandwiches to pack for the journey!

Extra gear:
- Scissors
- Tape or glue

What to do

1. Cut this page out of the book. Follow the guides to cut it into 15 strips.
2. Match up the letters to stick the strips together in the right order. Orange tabs with the same letter should overlap.
3. Starting from Neptune, roll the strip in a coil around a pencil. Get your sandwiches ready and unroll the paper to start your journey through the solar system.

WARNING! THIS PAGE WILL SELF-DESTRUCT!

The scale of your map will be one inch = 15,550,000 miles!

One naughty astronaut really did take a sandwich into space. NASA astronaut John Young snuck a corned beef sandwich into his spacesuit before he went into orbit in 1965. It was a bad idea—when he tried to eat it, crumbs began floating around the cabin threatening to damage the electronics!

Here are some things to think about on your journey. How do the distances between planets change as you travel through the solar system? How big would the Sun look from each planet? Are those alien spaceships between Mars and Jupiter, or just the asteroid belt?

Did you know that the planets don't travel in perfect circles around the Sun? They have elliptical orbits (a slightly squashed circle), so their distance from the Sun is always changing.

MERCURY

VENUS

EARTH

ASTEROID BELT

MARS

JUPITER

SATURN

URANUS

NEPTUNE

SUN

a b c d e f g h i j k l m n

10

HOW TO BUILD A UNIVERSE

Imagine squishing the 13.7-billion-year history of the universe into a single year. If the Big Bang happens right at the start, how long does it take for our planet to appear and fill up with plants, animals, and people?

Extra gear:
- Universe-in-a-Year cards (page 2)
- Scissors

What to do:
1. Cut out the cards on page 2. Each one is an event in the history of the universe.
2. If the universe was formed in a year, when do you think each event would happen? Place the cards on top of the corresponding calendar month, then check the inside of the back cover to see if you were right!

What would be happening on your birthday?

The year begins with the ultimate fireworks display—the Big Bang!

On this timescale, each month represents just over one billion years of cosmic history!

JANUARY
1 2 3 4 5 6 7
8 9 10 11 12 13 14
15 16 17 18 19 20 21
22 23 24 25 26 27 28
29 30 31

FEBRUARY
1 2 3 4 5 6 7
8 9 10 11 12 13 14
15 16 17 18 19 20 21
22 23 24 25 26 27 28
29

MARCH
1 2 3 4 5 6 7
8 9 10 11 12 13 14
15 16 17 18 19 20 21
22 23 24 25 26 27 28
29 30 31

APRIL
1 2 3 4 5 6 7
8 9 10 11 12 13 14
15 16 17 18 19 20 21
22 23 24 25 26 27 28
29 30

MAY
1 2 3 4 5 6 7
8 9 10 11 12 13 14
15 16 17 18 19 20 21
22 23 24 25 26 27 28
29 30 31

JUNE
1 2 3 4 5 6 7
8 9 10 11 12 13 14
15 16 17 18 19 20 21
22 23 24 25 26 27 28
29 30

JULY
1 2 3 4 5 6 7
8 9 10 11 12 13 14
15 16 17 18 19 20 21
22 23 24 25 26 27 28
29 30 31

AUGUST
1 2 3 4 5 6 7
8 9 10 11 12 13 14
15 16 17 18 19 20 21
22 23 24 25 26 27 28
29 30 31

SEPTEMBER
1 2 3 4 5 6 7
8 9 10 11 12 13 14
15 16 17 18 19 20 21
22 23 24 25 26 27 28
29 30

OCTOBER
1 2 3 4 5 6 7
8 9 10 11 12 13 14
15 16 17 18 19 20 21
22 23 24 25 26 27 28
29 30 31

NOVEMBER
1 2 3 4 5 6 7
8 9 10 11 12 13 14
15 16 17 18 19 20 21
22 23 24 25 26 27 28
29 30

DECEMBER
1 2 3 4 5 6 7
8 9 10 11 12 13 14
15 16 17 18 19 20 21
22 23 24 25 26 27 28
29 30 31

GRAVITY RACE

What's faster—this page, or your sneakers?
With your help, this page can win a gravity race!

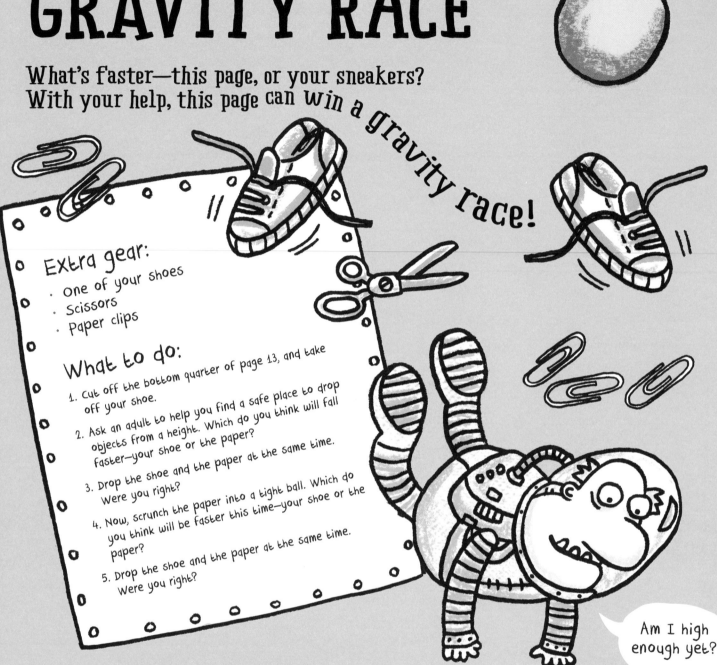

Extra gear:
- One of your shoes
- Scissors
- Paper clips

What to do:

1. Cut off the bottom quarter of page 13, and take off your shoe.

2. Ask an adult to help you find a safe place to drop objects from a height. Which do you think will fall faster—your shoe or the paper?

3. Drop the shoe and the paper at the same time. Were you right?

4. Now, scrunch the paper into a tight ball. Which do you think will be faster this time—your shoe or the paper?

5. Drop the shoe and the paper at the same time. Were you right?

Am I high enough yet?

Objects fall to the ground because of gravity. This is the "glue" that sticks our solar system together. It's not a sticky, gloopy glue, but an invisible force that pulls objects toward each other. Every object has a gravitational force, but we only notice the pull of massive objects such as planets. No matter where you drop an object on Earth, gravity will pull it toward the center of the planet.

To work like a scientist, make sure you are not dropping the objects onto someone's head!

This experiment proves that gravity makes all objects accelerate toward Earth at the same rate. Heavier things don't fall faster than lighter things. So what does change the speed of a falling object? Objects rub against the air as they fall. This "air resistance" is what slows objects down. A flat piece of paper has a greater surface area than a ball of paper, so the air resistance is greater.

NEVER drop a hammer on Earth!

WARNING! THIS PAGE WILL SELF-DESTRUCT!

For a fair test of gravity, you need to drop objects somewhere without air—such as the Moon! An astronaut once dropped a feather and a hammer on the Moon, then watched them hit the ground at the same time.

D

This piece of paper can put air resistance to work. Turn over to find out how.

Use this piece of paper for the gravity race!

What to do:

Put air resistance to work by making a paper helicopter!

1. Cut off the second quarter of page 14.

2. Cut along the solid lines.

3. Fold flaps A and B over flap C and hold them together at the bottom with a paper clip.

4. Fold flaps D and E in opposite directions to make blades.

5. Throw the helicopter into the air and see what happens.

Try dropping the helicopter and a paper clip at the same time. Which falls faster—the lighter paper clip, or the heavier helicopter?

A

D

C

B

E

COSMIC DUST

Don't look now, but a meteorite just landed in your garden!

Good places to collect micrometeorites:
· The middle of a desert
· Antarctica
· Your backyard

Extra gear:
· Tape
· Very strong magnet
· Modeling clay
· Plastic bag
· Glass jar or other container

What to do:

1. Choose a calm, dry day. Cut out the circle and strip below. Join the cut and dotted lines on the circle to make a cone.

2. Attach the strip of paper below the point of the cone in a loop and weigh it down with a lump of modeling clay. Pop the bottom of the cone into a heavy container such as a glass jar, and put it outside. Choose a high spot, away from roads, buildings, and trees.

3. Leave the cone for up to 48 hours. Bring it inside without disturbing the dust that has collected in it. Some of this dust is space dust!

4. To identify micrometeorites, pop a strong magnet into a plastic bag. Hold it on the inside of the cone and slowly pull it toward the top. Any dust or grit that travels with it is magnetic and may be a micrometeorite. Let these particles cling to the magnet and repeat.

5. Hold the magnet over a piece of white paper. Remove the magnet from the bag so the magnetic dust falls onto the paper.

6. Use cellophane tape to hold the particles in place, and examine them.

TEMPLATE

Every day, anywhere from five to a few hundred tons of micrometeorites plunge into Earth's atmosphere and fall to the ground. They don't leave craters. After a bumpy journey through the atmosphere, most are so micro you could line up six on a human hair. But some are big enough to collect.

WARNING! THIS PAGE WILL SELF-DESTRUCT!

What do you call a space rock that misses Earth?

A meteorwrong!

DON'T GET COSMIC DUST ON THE CARPET!

These tiny grains of rock were once whizzing around the solar system as part of a comet or asteroid. Collisions in space send chunks of rock hurtling toward Earth every day. Most burn up to nothing as they fall through the atmosphere, but some micrometeorites make it to the ground, at a rate of one per square yard per year. Every footstep you take outside will pick up grains of cosmic dust!

How did the astronaut keep up his pants?

With an asteroid belt!

WHY ARE METEORITES MAGNETIC?

Most space rocks contain a lot of magnetic metal, such as iron and nickel. This helps you tell them apart from other dust and grit in your garden, such as ash or pollen grains. Earth rocks can also be magnetic, so look out for these other signs too:

METEORITE CHECKLIST

Unless you are very lucky, the meteorites collected in your cone will be a few hundredths of an inch across! But bigger ones do land on Earth. Here's how to tell them apart from normal rocks.

☐ Magnetic

☐ Strangely lumpy

☐ Dark crust

☐ Very heavy for their size

POCKET ROCKET

This small but speedy rocket has all the right parts—a nose cone, rocket body, and fins for a smooth flight. You're just missing two million pounds of explosive fuel. But don't worry—

this rocket is launched

with puff power!

A real rocket is this shape—but 500 times bigger!

The body of a real rocket is not empty. It's full of rocket fuel, which is burned very quickly. Exhaust gases burst out of the bottom of the rocket, sending it in the opposite direction.

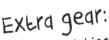

5, 4, 3, 2, 1 . . . Blast off!

WARNING! THIS PAGE WILL SELF-DESTRUCT!

Extra gear:
- Bendy drinking straw
- Pens or pencils
- Tape or glue
- Scissors

What to do:

1. Cut out the templates on this page.

2. Decorate each one. Don't forget to name your rocket, so it can be identified if it reaches the Moon!

3. Place a pen or pencil along the long edge of the rocket body. Roll the paper around it to make a long cylinder. Secure the paper cylinder with tape or glue, then slide the pen or pencil out.

4. Bend the nose cone template so the straight edges overlap. Hold in place with tape, then join the cone to the rocket body with tape or glue.

5. Join the fins to the rocket by bending the flaps in opposite directions and gluing them to the rocket body at the base.

6. Bend the straw, and slide the rocket onto the long end. Point the rocket towards the Moon and blow through the straw as hard as you can.

rocket body

nose cone

fin

glue

fin

fin

glue

glue

What do you think of that café on the Moon?

Great food, but it had no atmosphere!

WHY ARE ROCKETS SHAPED LIKE ROCKETS?

To leave Earth's atmosphere, a rocket has to beat the pull of gravity AND push a lot of air out of the way. A pointed nose cone pushes through the air more easily. The narrower the rocket, the less air it has to push out of the way. Because they are narrow, rockets also have to be very tall, to fit in all the fuel needed to blast them into space. The fins help the long, thin rocket to fly in the right direction without wobbling from side to side. Try launching your rocket with and without fins to see the difference!

Challenge your friends to a rocket race. How high or far can you make the rocket go?

rocket body

fin

glue

nose cone

glue

fin

glue

fin

glue

MOON DIARY

Most space exploration has been done by making careful observations from Earth. Keep a diary to get to the bottom of the Moon's mysterious shape-shifting.

Extra gear:
- Pencil

What to do:
1. Persuade your parents that you need to stay up late for a month—in the name of science!
2. Every night, look carefully at the Moon.
3. Shade the circles to record what you see.

Day 1

Day 2

Day 3

Day 4

Day 5

Day 6

Day 11

Day 10

Day 9

Day 8

Day 7

Day 12

Day 13

Day 14

Day 15

Day 16

Day 17

Day 18

Day 23

Day 22

Day 21

Day 20

Day 19

Day 24

Day 25

Day 26

Day 27

Day 28

Day 29

Day 30

DATA LOG

Cows jumping over the Moon

Men in the Moon

Moon rabbits

Big baboons combing their auburn hair

If you can't wait a month, zoom to page 37 to make a Moon flip book and see the whole cycle in a second.

19

WHAT'S HAPPENING?

The Moon doesn't really change shape—it's a trick of the light. Just like Earth, one side of the Moon is always bathed in sunlight. "Moonlight" is really sunlight bouncing off the Moon's surface. As the Moon orbits Earth, we see can see different amounts of the sunlit side. These different views are called phases.

Sometimes the entire sunlit side faces toward us (a full moon). Sometimes we only see part of the sunny side.

If you stood on the Moon, you'd see phases of the Earth!

The Moon spins as it orbits Earth, so the same side always faces Earth. Until the 1950s, no one knew what was on the other side. Abandoned alien spaceships? Cheese mines? When human spacecraft finally flew around the Moon their pictures showed that the far side of the Moon is . . . just like the near side!

I don't like the way you're looking at me.

It's just a phase.

NEW MOON

Earth's Moon is close enough for us to get a good look. Over thousands of years, people have imagined seeing different shapes in the dark and light patterns on the surface.

The light and dark areas are actually different types of rock. The light areas are the highlands, the oldest parts of the Moon's surface. The darker rock was formed by lava that flowed into dips and dents on the Moon's surface. These areas are known as "seas."

Face

Hands

Rabbit

Frog

What shapes can you see in the Moon? Record them here.

Why didn't you park on the Moon?

It was full.

DON'T GET DAZZLED

The Sun is a star, but it's much closer to Earth than the stars you can see at night—close enough to damage your eyes if you look at it. This pinhole viewer will help you take a safe look at the Sun.

NEVER

look at the sun directly, or through any kind of binoculars or telescope. Sunlight can damage your eyes forever, and even cause blindness.

Extra gear:
- Scissors
- Glue or tape
- Thumbtack

What to do:

1. Cut out the template on the next page and fold along the dashed lines. Cut out the rectangular hole on one side.

2. Use a thumbtack to make a small hole at the center of the cross.

3. Fold the paper into a square tube, gluing or taping the tabs in place. Make sure there are no small gaps at the ends.

4. Follow the instructions on the side of the viewer to see the Sun safely.

WHAT AM I LOOKING AT?

A 4.5-billion-year-old star! Like all stars, the Sun is a huge ball of superheated gas. Nuclear reactions at the center make huge amounts of energy. This energy escapes from the Sun's surface and zooms across space, hitting Earth eight minutes later!

SUN SECRETS

Satellites can get a close look at the Sun without hurting their eyes. They have recorded enormous explosions on the surface, bubbles of plasma that erupt into space, and solar quakes that ripple across the surface.

WARNING! THIS PAGE WILL SELF-DESTRUCT!

NOW YOU SEE IT, NOW YOU DON'T

The Sun is 400 times bigger than the Moon. Because the Sun is almost 400 times farther away, they look about the same size from Earth. This means that when a full Moon gets between Earth and the Sun, it blocks the Sun's light and causes an eclipse.

TOTAL ECLIPSE—The Moon is perfectly in line with the Sun. It covers the whole Sun and the sky gets dark.

ANNULAR ECLIPSE—The Moon covers the center of the Sun, but a "ring of fire" is visible around the edge.

PARTIAL ECLIPSE—The Moon only covers part of the Sun.

How does the Sun keep his hat on?

Eclipse it!

1. Stand with your back to the Sun.

2. Hold the viewer near your forehead, with the pinhole pointing back over your head towards the Sun.

3. Look through the rectangular viewing hole. Adjust the position of the tube until you can see an image of the Sun on the end of the tube opposite the pinhole.

WARNING: Never look at the Sun directly, or through the pinhole.

A longer tube will give you a larger, clearer image of the Sun. Once you have gotten the hang of making a pinhole viewer, try making a six-foot-long version using cardboard boxes!

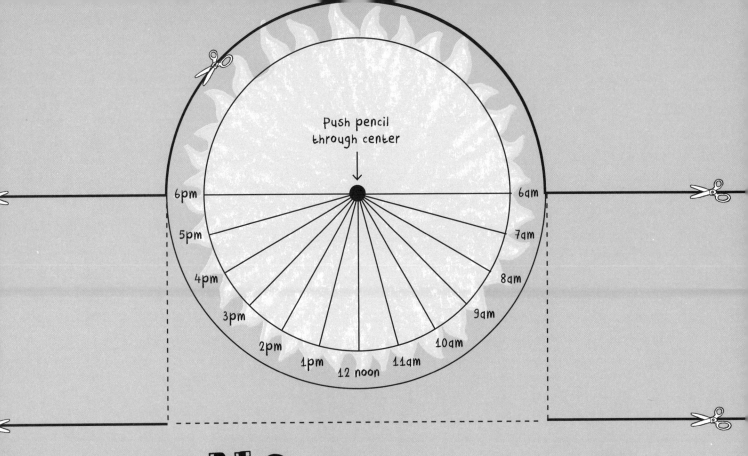

Push pencil through center

6pm
5pm
4pm
3pm
2pm
1pm
12 noon
11am
10am
9am
8am
7am
6am

KEEPING TIME

As our planet spins in space, the Sun seems to move across the sky. The direction of shadows cast by the Sun changes during the day, giving us a really handy way to tell the time!

HOW FAST AM I MOVING WHEN I'M SITTING STILL?

The Earth spins 15° every hour (this is why the hour lines on your sundial are 15° apart). This means that the land at the Equator is moving at 1,041 miles per hour. At the same time, the planet is zooming around the Sun at about 1,110 miles per hour.

WARNING! THIS PAGE WILL SELF-DESTRUCT!

Next time someone asks you to sit still, explain that it's impossible!

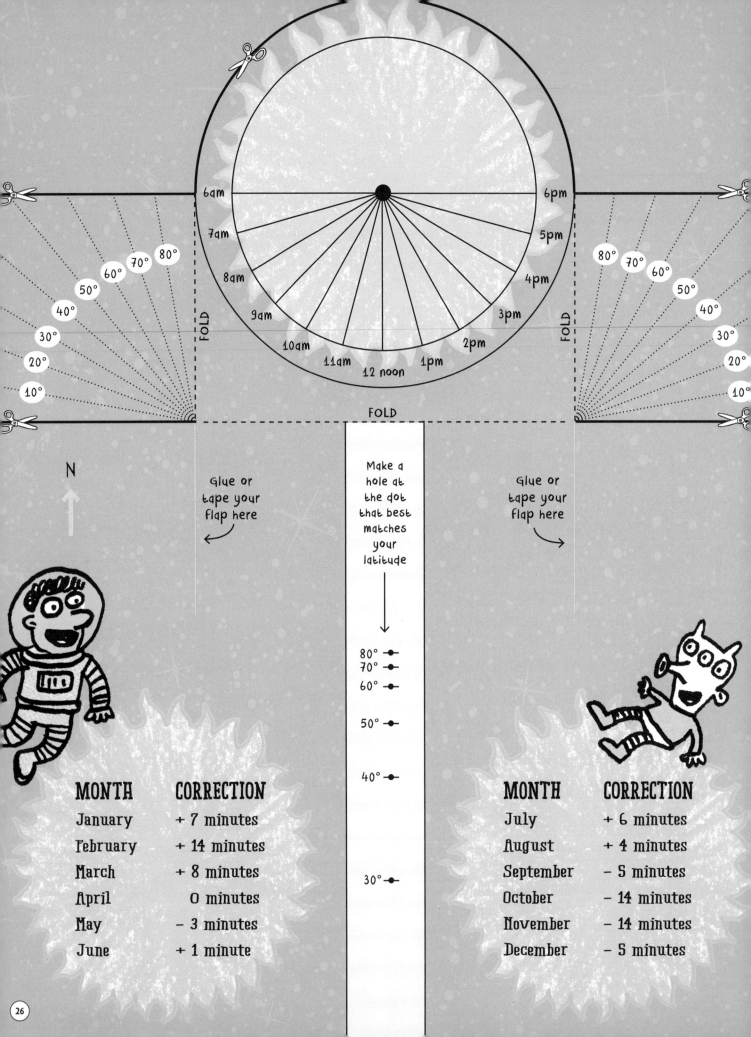

6am 7am 8am 9am 10am 11am 12 noon 1pm 2pm 3pm 4pm 5pm 6pm

FOLD

FOLD

FOLD

80° 70° 60° 50° 40° 30° 20° 10°

80° 70° 60° 50° 40° 30° 20° 10°

N

Glue or tape your flap here

Glue or tape your flap here

Make a hole at the dot that best matches your latitude

80°
70°
60°
50°
40°
30°

MONTH	CORRECTION
January	+ 7 minutes
February	+ 14 minutes
March	+ 8 minutes
April	0 minutes
May	– 3 minutes
June	+ 1 minute

MONTH	CORRECTION
July	+ 6 minutes
August	+ 4 minutes
September	– 5 minutes
October	– 14 minutes
November	– 14 minutes
December	– 5 minutes

Extra gear:

- Piece of corrugated cardboard
- Tape
- Scissors
- Sharp pencil
- Internet (to look up your latitude)
- Compass (optional)

What to do:

1. Remove page 25 from the book and cut along the solid lines.

2. Turn the paper over, and fold along the dashed lines.

3. Fold each small flap along the dotted line that best matches your latitude (how far you are from the Equator). You can look this up on the Internet.

4. Line up the folds you have made with the orange lines on the base, and glue or tape each small flap to the base.

5. Carefully push a sharp pencil through the center of the circle. Push the pointed end of the pencil down into the cardboard through the dot that best matches your latitude. The pencil is the gnomon of your sundial—the part that will cast shadows.

6. Place your sundial outside on a flat surface, with the arrow pointing true North. You can find this by looking at a map of your home or using a compass.

> You can adjust your readings using the table—or just tell everyone you are now on solar time!

2.

3.

4.

5.

6.

The sundial measures "solar time," or the position of the Sun in the sky. "Clock time" divides the world into artificial time zones to make life easier. Unless you live right at the center of your time zone, your sundial reading will be slightly different from clock time. The Sun's position in the sky also changes with the seasons, which affects the sundial reading by up to 15 minutes.

GET READY FOR YOUR SPACEWALK!

Spacesuits don't just keep astronauts warm. They are life support systems, communications modules, and personal jetpacks rolled into one! How quickly can you get this astronaut dressed for her spacewalk?

Extra gear:
- Scissors

What to do:
1. Cut out the astronaut and the spacesuit layers.
2. Follow the checklist to dress your astronaut for space, folding the tabs around the astronaut.

CHECKLIST

- [x] Maximum Absorption Garment
- [x] Liquid Cooling and Ventilation Garment
- [/] Lower Torso Assembly
- [ ] Hard Upper Torso
- [ ] Arms
- [ ] Displays and Control Module (front)

- [ ] Primary Life Support System (back)
- [ ] Communications Carrier Assembly
- [ ] Helmet
- [ ] Visor Assembly
- [ ] Gloves
- [ ] Tethers

What did the astronaut get in his socks?

Black holes.

The arms attach separately to the HUT.

Gloves allow astronauts to move their fingers and wrists. Fingertip heaters help keep their hands warm.

The Communications Carrier Assembly (CCA) is a cap with earphones and microphones built in.

The Helmet is a plastic bubble, which seals to the neck of the HUT.

The Visor Assembly has three different visors. Headlamps and cameras can also be attached.

The Displays and Control Module is mounted on the astronaut's chest.

The Primary Life Support System (PLSS) is worn on the back, like a backpack. It has breathing equipment, a battery, water-cooling equipment, a fan, a two-way radio, and a warning system.

DON'T FORGET THE ACCESSORIES!

The cuff checklist has a list of the tasks for a spacewalk.

A wrist mirror lets the astronaut see the controls on their chest.

Safety tethers attach the astronaut to the spacecraft. It's just not cool to float off . . .

This drink bag clips inside the HUT.

MARTIAN BUGS

These creepy bugs seem to move with a mind of their own! Keep your friends guessing at the secret to their extraterrestrial flip-Flopping.

Extra gear:

- Scissors
- Marbles or large ball bearings (one per bug)
- Tape or glue
- Colored markers

What to do:

1. Cut out the net for each bug. (A "net" is a flat shape that folds up to make a 3D object—such as a cube, a pyramid . . . or an alien bug from Mars!).
2. Color the back of the bug.
3. Turn the paper over and fold along the dotted lines.
4. Bring the sides together, and glue the tabs marked A together.
5. Curve tab B around the end of the bug, and glue or tape it to B.
6. Add the secret ingredient—a marble.
7. Curve tab C around the other end, and glue or tape it to C.
8. Stick on the legs and antennae.

WARNING! THIS PAGE WILL SELF-DESTRUCT!

BUG 1 BODY

BUG 1 LEGS

BUG 1 ANTENNA

BUG 2 BODY

BUG 2 LEGS

BUG 2 ANTENNA

WHAT'S HAPPENING?

When the bug (or the surface it's on) is tilted, the marble rolls around inside. As it crashes into the curved ends, the bug flips over—leaving the marble free to roll again. The bugs move in a random way, which makes them fun to race. It's impossible to predict which bug will win!

What do you call an alien with three eyes?

An aliiien!

ARE THERE BURPING BUGS ON MARS?

Robot rovers and space probes have been hunting for signs that microbes once lived on Mars. They have found evidence that there was once water on the red planet. This is exciting, because all living things need water. A Mars rover has also detected methane—a gas burped by living things on Earth! Does this mean there are burping bugs on Mars, or does the methane come from something else?

Try out your bug by putting it down on a slightly tilted surface. It will move like it's crossing the rocky craters of Mars.

BUG 1 LEGS

BUG 1 BODY

BACK

B

C

A
Blue-glue

BUG 2 LEGS

B

C

BUG 2 BODY

A
Blue-glue

BACK

BUG 1 ANTENNA

BUG 2 ANTENNA

STUCK ON YOU

Thrown off balance by Earth's tilted axis? Seasons got you in a spin?
Make this flip book and watch a year go by in the blink of an eye!

Extra gear:
- Scissors
- Stapler

What to do:

1. Cut out the 24 cards on page 38. Stack them sunny-side-down from 1 to 24.

2. Staple them together at the left-hand edge on the dotted line.

3. Hold the stapled edge in your left hand and flick through the pictures with your right thumb to see Earth orbit the sun.

4. Flip the book over to watch our view of the Moon change as it orbits Earth.

Earth is tilted on its axis, meaning that each hemisphere is tilted toward the Sun for part of the year (summer) and away from the Sun for part of the year (winter). The hemisphere that tilts toward the Sun gets more sunlight, so it is warmer at that time of year.

I'm actually 40 years old on Mercury!

A year is the time it takes for a planet to orbit its star once. Every birthday, you celebrate another 584-million-mile trip around the Sun! If you think 365 days is too long to wait, move to Mercury, where you'd be blowing out birthday candles every three months!

MOON MUDDLE

Scientists have spotted more than 170 moons orbiting planets and dwarf planets. Don't be fooled by their second-rate status—moons are some of the most interesting places in the solar system.

See if you can untangle the moon muddle to match the moons to the facts. Turn to the inside back cover to check your answers.

CALLISTO

E Has twice as much water as Earth, hidden in underground oceans

GANYMEDE

F Is home to one of the chilliest spots in the solar system

D Reflects just 12% of the sunlight that hits it

EUROPA

A An icy crust makes this moon the smoothest object in the Solar System

G Has lakes, rivers, and seas filled with liquid methane (natural gas), complete with methane clouds and marble-size drops of methane rain

EARTH'S MOON

C Is bigger than Mercury

B Is wrapped in orange smog

TRITON

TITAN

MIRANDA

H
In some parts of this moon, it has been snowing for tens of millions of years

ENCELADUS

I
Orbits Mars twice in a Martian day

J
More than 300 active volcanoes blast sulphur dioxide into space . . . which falls back down as yellow snow that smells of rotten eggs!

K
Has canyons so deep that it would take you ten minutes to reach the bottom if you fell in

L
Has an atmosphere that is mainly nitrogen, like Earth

IO

IAPETUS

PLUTO

N
Reflects almost 100% of the sunlight that hits it

M
Has mountains made of ice

P
Is so cold that nitrogen freezes and falls as pink snow

O
Has lakes of molten lava

PHOBOS

Q
Has one dazzling white, and one deep black side

MERCURY

S
Has geysers that spew water hundreds of miles into space

R
Has huge sand dunes

TITANIA

LUNARLYMPICS

It's time to find out how well you would run, jump, and throw on the Moon. The Moon has only a little more than 1% of the Earth's mass, so its gravity is much weaker. Around six times weaker!

EVENT ONE—THE HIGH BOUNCE

Stand next to a wall. Hold a piece of chalk in one hand and mark how high you can reach while standing on the floor. Now jump as high as you can and mark where your hand reaches.

inches

MY BEST
EARTH JUMP

· · · · · · · · · · · · · · · X 6 · · · · · · · · · · · · · · · →

inches

MY BEST
MOON JUMP

EVENT TWO—THE LONG KICK

Mark a spot on the ground, and put the soccer ball on it. Kick it as far as you can, and measure the distance it travels.

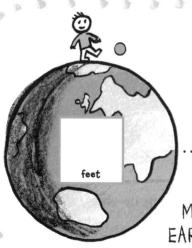

feet

MY BEST
EARTH KICK

· · · · · · · · · · · · · · · X 6 · · · · · · · · · · · · · · · →

feet

MY BEST
MOON KICK

EVENT THREE—WEIGHTLIFTING

Ask a friend to sit on a scale. Write down their starting weight in pounds. Now take hold of their arms and pull up as hard as you can. Write down the lowest weight that appears on the scales and subtract it from the starting weight.

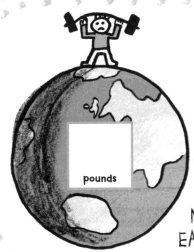

pounds

$\cdots\cdots\cdots\cdots\cdots\cdots\cdots\cdots$ X 6 $\cdots\cdots\cdots\cdots\cdots\cdots\cdots\rightarrow$

MY BEST
EARTH LIFT

pounds

MY BEST
MOON LIFT

Replace the 6 in each calculation with these numbers to calculate what would happen if the Lunarlympics was held elsewhere!

MERCURY	2.6
VENUS	1.1
MARS	2.6
JUPITER	0.4
SATURN	0.9
URANUS	1.1
NEPTUNE	0.9

How do you say sorry on the Moon?

Just Apollo-gize!

WHAT WOULD IT BE LIKE TO LIVE ON THE MOON?

Not a lot happens on the Moon when there are no astronauts around. There is no flowing water and no wind to disturb the dusty surface. The Moon spins very slowly in space, with 14 Earth days between dawn and dusk. During the long nights, temperatures dip as low as −413 degrees Fahrenheit—some of the lowest in the solar system! There's no chance of rain, but don't put that umbrella away—the Moon's thin atmosphere means that meteorites as big as golf balls rain down on the surface.

BEDROOM PLANETARIUM

How many stars can you count on a dark night?

Millions?

Billions?

The answer is around 4,500 with your eyes alone. Grab a pair of binoculars, and this goes up to more than 200,000! To keep track, ancient astronomers used constellations.

Extra gear:
- Thumbtack or sharp pencil
- Old, clean cardboard tube
- Cork or foam mat
- Scissors
- Elastic band
- Flashlight

What to do:
1. Remove the opposite page from the book and lay it face up on a cork or foam mat. Carefully poke a hole through each star.
2. Cut out each circle, and cut slits around the edge. Fold the tabs over a cardboard tube. Use an elastic band to hold it in place.
3. When it's dark, shine a flashlight through the tube to project the constellation onto a wall or ceiling.

Project these constellations onto a ceiling to make a personal planetarium!

STORYBOOK IN THE STARS

The constellations are 88 imaginary shapes connecting stars in the same patch of sky. Many were created by the ancient Greeks and Romans, whose stories of the battles between monsters and heroes helped people remember the patterns. They obviously thought the skies were less peaceful than they look!

The stars that we can see from Earth change over the course of a year, so constellations were a useful way to track the seasons. They also helped astronomers share their discoveries. "Look at the end of the Great Bear's tail," is a lot quicker than saying, "Check out the 701st star from the left. . . . Left a bit . . . Right a bit . . . Oh, I give up!"

Once you've practiced spotting constellations on your ceiling, it'll be a cinch to spot them in the night sky. The stars that you see in the sky depend on where you are on Earth and what time of year it is.

Why doesn't the Dog Star laugh when you tickle it?

It's too Sirius.

The names of the constellations are still used, but they refer to 88 patches of sky rather than the shapes themselves.

CENTAURUS / THE CENTAUR
In Greek myths, the centaur had the head and torso of a man attached to the body of a horse.

ANDROMEDA
Andromeda was a princess who was chained to a rock as a sea monster's supper, but rescued.

URSA MAJOR / THE GREAT BEAR
Seven of its stars make up a famous pattern called the Big Dipper.

ORION / THE HUNTER
Orion was a great hunter in Greek myths. The line of three stars in the middle is called Orion's belt.

LEO / THE LION
This was the lion that Hercules wrestled.

HERCULES
Hercules was a super-strong Greek hero who battled with many beasts. In his constellation, he is standing on the head of a dragon!

CETUS / THE SEA MONSTER
This was the sea monster sent to eat Andromeda.

SCORPIUS / THE SCORPION
After Orion boasted that he could kill any wild animal, this scorpion was sent to finish him off!

PEGASUS / THE WINGED HORSE
Pegasus was a winged horse that helped a Greek hero to kill a fire-breathing monster.

STAR SCRIBBLES

Everything in the universe is moving and changing. Stars die and new stars are formed all the time, so the constellations are not fixed. In thousands of years, new constellations will be needed. Get a head start by designing your own!

Extra gear:
· Pen or pencil

What to do:
This is a map of stars visible from the Northern Hemisphere. Be like an ancient astronomer and join the dots to create a new constellation.

Our Sun won't die for another five billion years—just enough time to pick up your room!

Give your constellation a name and a legend.

NAME: ....

LEGEND: ....
....
....
....
....

47

If you stand in a different place on Earth, you'll see a different set of constellations! This is a map of stars visible from the Southern Hemisphere.

Give your constellation a name and a legend.

NAME: ....

LEGEND: ....

....

....

....

....

What's an astronaut's favorite key on a keyboard?

The space bar!

GALAXY GENERATOR

A galaxy is a huge, spinning group of stars, dust, and gas, held together by gravity. Grab some scissors and glue, and turn this page into a beautiful spiral galaxy!

Pattern

Extra gear:
- Scissors
- Glue
- Tape
- Small piece of silver foil

What to do:

1. Cut out the base, and carefully cut the hole from the center.

2. Put the base front down over the pattern and hold it in place with masking tape.

3. Cut out the 45 small strips of paper, keeping them in numbered piles.

4. Dab some glue onto the blue area of the base, and stick the first strip of paper in place over the area of the pattern marked with a 1 and a *. Then glue a strip marked 2 in the spot marked 2 next to the first strip. Work your way around the base counterclockwise, centering strips from each group over the right numbers on the pattern. Make sure you don't glue the strips to the pattern—just the base.

5. Keep adding strips until you reach the middle. Glue the piece of foil over the hole. Remove the pattern.

6. Cover the back of the strips with tape. Finally, cut around the dashed line to trim the spiral galaxy into a circular shape.

WARNING! THIS PAGE WILL SELF-DESTRUCT!

BACK

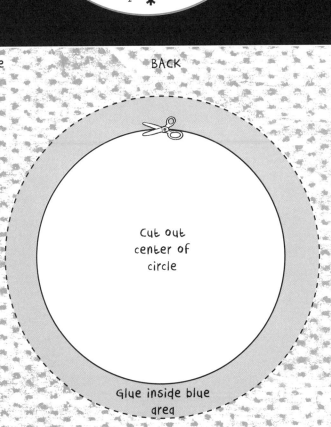

Cut out center of circle

Glue inside blue area

Almost three-quarters of the galaxies that can be seen from Earth are spiral galaxies, with long arms spiraling out from a bright bulge at the center. Our own galaxy, the Milky Way, is a spiral galaxy.

Where would you find an alien with no legs?

Where you left it.

Make more spiral galaxies in the same way, and hang them in your bedroom planetarium!

Our Sun takes about 250 million years to make one orbit of the Milky Way, taking Earth and the other planets along for the ride. The last time Earth was this side of the galaxy, it was dinosaurs, not humans, enjoying the view!

5 5 5 5 5 5 5 5 5

4 4 4 4 4 4 4 4 4

3 3 3 3 3 3 3 3 3

2 2 2 2 2 2 2 2 2

1 1 1 1 1 1 1 1 1

Front

Cut out center of circle

STEP RIGHT THROUGH

Have you ever wished you could leap through a wormhole into another world, like they do in science fiction films? Warm up by learning to leap through this page!*

WARNING! THIS PAGE WILL SELF-DESTRUCT!

*You might not find another world on the other side, but you will amaze your friends.

Extra gear:

Scissors

What to do:

It's one small step . . .

1. Start by tearing this page out of the book. Fold it in half along the dotted black line.

2. Cut along the solid black lines—do not cut all the way to the edge.

3. You now have lots of mini folds. Leave the first and last folds intact, but cut through the others to make a big hole.

4. Open out the hole and step right through!

← DON'T CUT THIS FOLD

← Cut the dotted folds between the stars.

← Cut the dotted folds between the stars.

← DON'T CUT THIS FOLD

WHAT'S A WORMHOLE?

It's a shortcut through space and time—in theory! Space scientists think wormholes could be formed when space gets bent or distorted, bringing two distant points together (a bit like bringing opposite ends of this page together by bending the paper in half). Wormholes sound exciting because they could make it possible to travel huge distances and explore different solar systems. But scientists haven't yet found proof that they really exist.

SLURP!

SPIT!

Einstein came up with a theory about space.

About time, too.

Once you've learned how, try the trick with a smaller piece of paper. Can you leap through a birthday card or a bus ticket?

Challenge your friends to see who can fit the most people inside the perimeter of a tiny piece of paper. Use this trick to win every time!

MIND THE BLACK HOLE!

Watch out—you're being sucked toward a black hole at the center of a spiral galaxy.

Will you be stretched into space-spaghetti, or burned to a crisp?

Extra gear:
- Scissors
- Thin cardboard
- Two game pieces
- Dice
- A fellow astronaut

What to do:

1. Take this page out of the book and glue or tape it to a piece of thin cardboard with the game board face up. Remember to read the rest of this side first!

2. Carefully cut out the six wormholes. Balance the cardboard on top of a box, so that the game pieces can fall through the wormholes.

3. Follow the instructions on the game board to play.

Scientists think there is a supermassive black hole at the center of most galaxies—including the Milky Way. The bigger the bulge at the center of a galaxy, the bigger the black hole! Black holes are strange areas of space where an enormous gravitational pull squeezes matter into a tiny area. The gravitational pull is so strong, not even light can escape. Like whirlpools, swirling discs of space dust and stars surround black holes.

CRISP OR SPAGHETTI?

Scientists can't see black holes—just their effects on nearby objects. No one is completely sure what happens to objects that get sucked in. An astronaut who got too close might be stretched into spaghetti by the gravitational pull, or burned to a crisp by a superheated "firewall" of energy. Either way, you wouldn't have long to worry about it— you'd be crushed once you got to the core!

It's hard to choose!

How to play

Two players

1. Put your game pieces on the starting positions at the edges of the galaxy.

2. Take turns rolling the dice and moving.

3. If you land on a symbol, follow the instructions.

4. The winner is the astronaut who avoids being sucked into the black hole!

 Dazzled by a supernova, miss a turn

Gravity boost, move the number of spaces shown

Fallen into a wormhole, start again

 CUT OUT BEFORE PLAY

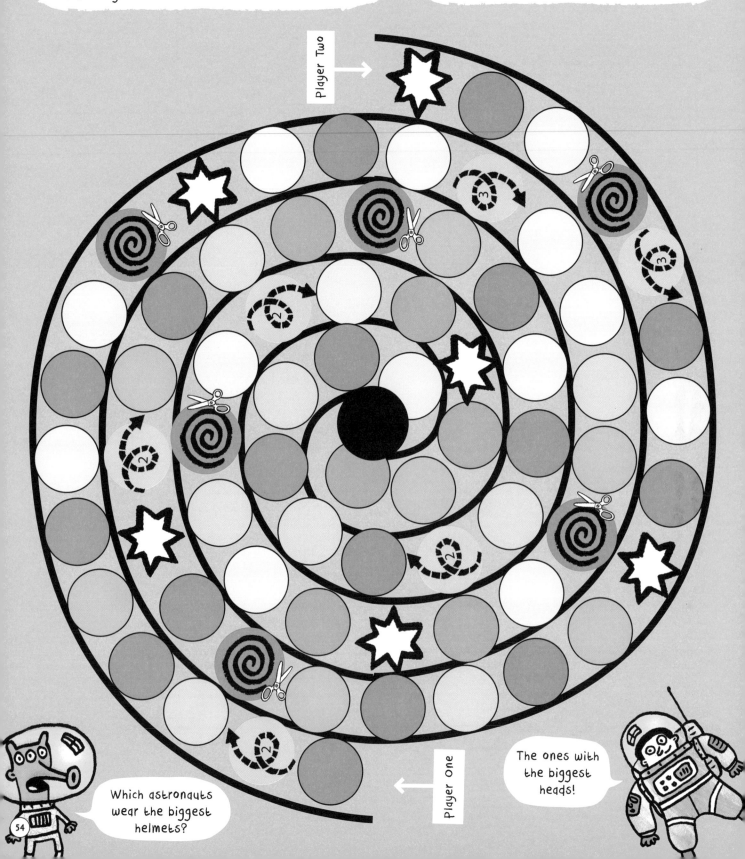

Player Two

Player One

Which astronauts wear the biggest helmets?

The ones with the biggest heads!

54

UNIDENTIFIED FLYING OBJECTS

UFO stands for Unidentified Flying Object. People often think they are alien spacecraft, but many "sightings" have actually been hoaxes. Make your own UFO and see if you can take photographs that fool your family!

Extra gear:
- Scissors
- Tape

WARNING!
THIS PAGE WILL
SELF-DESTRUCT!

Earth is home to the only life in the universe . . . that we know about. But the universe is so humongous, space scientists think there must be TONS more planets out there with conditions perfect for life. No wonder everyone gets so excited when they spot a UFO!

Space scientists think there may be up to 160 billion planets in our galaxy alone!

If any aliens are visiting Earth, they've come a long way. The next-nearest star to our Sun is 25 trillion miles away.

A racing car at top speed would take more than 12 million years to make the trip—not allowing for any bathroom breaks!

What do you call the alien spaceship that flew into the Sun?

An unidentified frying object!

55

What to do:

1. Cut out the eight squares and the dome template.

2. Fold the first square diagonally along the long dotted line.

3. Fold along the short dotted line to bring the right hand corner to the point. Repeat with the other squares.

4. Tuck the long point of one shape inside the small triangle-shaped flap of another. Repeat until you have joined all the shapes in a circle.

5. Turn the circle over and fold up the top flap of each shape. Use tape to hold the shapes firmly together.

6. Curve the edges of the dome template together and join them with tape. Stick this dome to the top of your UFO.

7. Throw the UFO into the air and try to snap a picture as it spins.

Dome template

56

ALIEN ID

Aliens are out there—but what do they look like? Creatures living in Earth's most extreme environments could give us clues.

POMPEII WORM

These worms are the most heat-tolerant animals on Earth. They live right next to hydrothermal vents on the sea floor, and are often spotted with their tails dangling in 175-degree-Fahrenheit water—do NOT try this at home.

BLOBFISH

Blobfish live in deep oceans, where the pressure is up to 120 times greater than it is at the surface. Its jelly-like blob of a body helps it float above the sea floor without being crushed.

HIMALAYAN JUMPING SPIDER

These tiny spiders live in mountains 22 thousand feet above sea level, higher than almost any other animal in the world. This means they can cope with very low oxygen levels.

YETI CRAB

Yeti crabs don't have eyes—there's no point in the darkness of the world's deepest oceans. Instead of hunting for food, they grow their own "gardens" of bacteria on their bristly claws.

DEEP-SEA AMPHIPOD

These super-sized shrimps live in deep ocean trenches, where the pressure would crush a human. Tough stomachs help them digest junk that sinks to the bottom, including wood from shipwrecks.

COCKROACH

These insects are so good at adapting to different conditions, they have been on Earth for more than 300 million years. They can survive huge doses of radiation, one of the biggest hazards in space.

SPINOLORICUS CINZIA

These mysterious creatures survive in a "dead zone" at the bottom of an ocean. Unlike every other animal on Earth, they live without any oxygen at all.

GIANT TUBE WORM

These 6-foot-long worms live near hydrothermal vents, where water heated by molten rock gushes out of the ocean floor. This water is full of chemicals that would kill most living things.

SAHARAN SILVER ANT

These ants survive in the world's hottest desert, sprinting out of their burrows to take advantage of an all-you-can-eat buffet of insects that have been killed by the extreme heat!

TARDIGRADE

These incredible creatures have come back to life after being heated above 300 degrees Fahrenheit and below -450 degrees Fahrenheit. Tardigrades were sent to space for ten days—without space suits—and were still happily going about their business when they came back to Earth!

SEA PIG

This animal is actually a type of sea cucumber! It feasts on mud and dead animals at the bottom of the world's deepest area of ocean, the Mariana Trench.

All these creatures live in conditions that would kill most living things—conditions like those on other planets and moons of the solar system. Scientists call them extremophiles.

Design your own alien life form, using features from Earth's extremophiles!

Alien ID:
Home planet or moon:
Habitat:

HOW HIGH?

This page will help you reach new heights—make an astrolabe and measure a skyscraper without leaving the ground!

Astrolabes were the first tools used by sailors to figure out where on Earth they were, using stars millions of miles away! On a clear night, tilt your astrolabe so you can see the North Star (Polaris) through the straw. The angle on your astrolabe is also your latitude!

Extra gear:
- Scissors
- Drinking straw
- Tape
- Paper clip
- About 8 inches of thread

What to do:
1. Cut out the astrolabe template inside the back cover of this book.

2. Cut a 4-inch piece of drinking straw. Place it across the flaps at the top of the astrolabe. Bend the flaps around the straw and tape them in place.

3. Cut a small notch in the corner of the astrolabe, in the place shown. Fit the thread into the notch and tie it in place.

4. Trim the thread so it is around 5 inches long and tie the paper clip onto the end. Your astrolabe is ready to use!

How do you serve tea in space?

On flying saucers!

stick tabs over the straw

straw

Write the measured angle here

Write the height from the ground to your eye here

Height

Distance

Write the distance from your feet to the building here

You can use your astrolabe to measure the height of anything—you just need to know how far you are from the object. A map can help you find out.

1. Line up the straw so you can see the top of the building through it. When the thread comes to rest, hold it against the card and read the angle.

2. Find your measured angle in the table, and write the number next to it in this box:

3. Now grab a calculator and do this speedy sum:

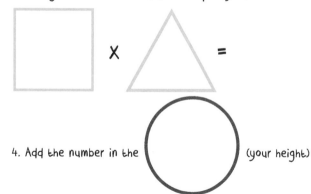

X =

4. Add the number in the (your height)

to your answer to reveal the height of the building!
Now, where's that ladder . . .

TANGENT TABLE

ANGLE		ANGLE	
5	0.0875	50	1.1918
10	0.1763	55	1.4281
15	0.2679	60	1.7321
20	0.3640	65	2.1445
25	0.4663	70	2.7475
30	0.5773	75	3.7321
35	0.7002	80	5.6713
40	0.8391	85	11.430
45	1		

SPACE JUNK

How long can you stay in orbit around Earth without

crashing into space junk

or bashing into

an asteroid?

Extra gear:
- Game pieces
- Dice
- Two or more players

What to do:

1. Put the game board on a flat surface. Launch your game pieces from Earth (in the center) by rolling the dice and following the numbered path.

2. Once you are in orbit, move from place to place by rolling the dice and following the numbered path.

3. If you crash into a piece of space junk, you must roll again to avoid it. If you land on Earth, the Moon, or the International Space Station, you can skip a turn while resting in a safe place. If you crash into an asteroid, you are out!

4. The winner is the last player left in orbit.

SUPERSONIC SCRAP

Millions of pieces of space junk are whizzing around Earth right now. They include old satellites, used-up bits of rocket, debris from crashes in space, and anything that astronauts have accidentally dropped during spacewalks. Like other orbiting objects, space junk travels at up to 17,500 miles per hour—more than 22 times the speed of sound! At that speed, even a small speck of paint can damage a spacecraft or satellite. To keep astronauts and the International Space Station safe, NASA tracks half a million pieces of space junk that are larger than marbles.

THE RULES

1. If you crash into a piece of space junk, roll again.
2. If you land on Earth, the Moon, or the International Space Station, skip a turn.
3. If you crash into an asteroid, you are out!

You made it to the Moon. SKIP A TURN!

START

Moon

Asteroid

Space Junk

Space station

SPACED OUT

This page morphs into a "Do Not Disturb" sign for guaranteed peace and quiet while you're busy destroying this book!

Extra gear:
- Scissors
- Two photographs of you, trimmed to $2\frac{1}{2}$ x $2\frac{1}{2}$ inches

What to do:

1. Cut out the template, including the center shapes.

2. Glue your photographs face down in the places shown.

3. Fold along the dotted line and glue the sides together.

WARNING! THIS PAGE WILL SELF-DESTRUCT!

Cut out center

Cut out center

DO NOT ENTER

ENTER WITH CAUTION

Cut out center

WARNING:
Self-Destructing
Science in Progress

Cut out center

Self-Destructing
Science in Progress